ANIMAL HELPERS

Ben Hubbard and Sara Ugolotti

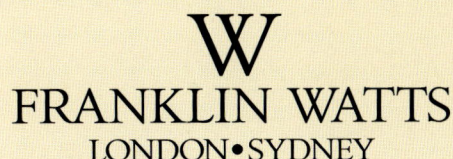

FRANKLIN WATTS
LONDON • SYDNEY

First published in Great Britain in 2025 by Hodder and Stoughton
© Hodder and Stoughton Ltd 2025

All rights reserved

Managing editor: Victoria Brooker / Design: Peter Scoulding

ISBN: 9781445190723 (hbk)
ISBN: 9781445190747 (pbk)
ISBN: 9781445190730 (ebk)

Printed and bound in China

Franklin Watts, an imprint of Hachette Children's Group
Part of Hodder and Stoughton
Carmelite House, 50 Victoria Embankment, London EC4Y 0DZ

An Hachette UK Company

www.hachette.co.uk
www.hachettechildrens.co.uk

The authorised representative in the EEA is Hachette Ireland, 8 Castlecourt Centre, Dublin 15, D15 XTP3, Ireland (email: info@hbgi.ie)

CONTENTS

Amazing Animals	4	Global Warming Whales	28
Pet Teams	6	Disease Detectors	30
Animal Guides	8	Space Animals	32
Hearing Dogs	10	Alert Animals	34
Pet Therapy	12	Herding Dogs	36
Pulling Ploughs	14	Ferret Electricians	38
Pack Animals	16	Animal Predictors	40
Camel Caravans	18	Animals Helping Animals	42
Sled Dogs	20	Humans Helping Animals	44
Rescue Horses	22	Glossary	46
Mountain Dogs	24	Further Information	47
Bomb Detection Bees	26	Index	48

AMAZING ANIMALS

Animals have been helping humans for thousands of years. Since ancient times, they have toiled with farmers in their fields and transported people and their goods. Animals have also been our loyal friends and companions; for many people, their pet is simply another member of the family.

For people with disabilities, animals are more than just pets. Instead, they are essential helpers that use their eyes and ears to help give their owners independence.

Other animals can provide therapy for those suffering from poor health. Just being around a friendly animal can bring a smile to people having a hard time, and help them feel better.

Animals are even more amazing than most people realise. With their super-senses and special abilities, animals can sniff out disease in humans, dig out those trapped by avalanches and even detect earthquakes before they strike. It's hard to imagine where humans would be without animals to help us.

PET TEAMS

The first animals to live with people were wild dogs that were descended from wolves. The dogs would hang around campfires at night and wait for scraps of food. Over time, they became domesticated, or tame, and went on to develop into different breeds.

Now we have all kinds of pets: snakes, stick insects, tarantulas and hedgehogs are just some of them. Whatever the animal, a pet quickly becomes a good friend. We look after our pets and make sure they are safe and healthy; and they look after us, too.

Cats can hear things far away and even sense earthquakes before we can. Horses can act as the eyes for people with impaired vision. Together, people and pets can make a great team.

Pets relax us and keep us company. But they also keep us safe by using their amazing senses. Dogs can smell many things we cannot and quickly warn us of danger.

ANIMAL GUIDES

Visually-impaired people have been helped by guide dogs since the 1930s. A guide dog acts as the owner's eyes, leading them while out walking and making sure they do not run into danger. But dogs are not the only guide animals helping people – miniature horses do the job, too.

Miniature horses are around the size of a large dog and perfect for people who are allergic to dog hair. The horses have excellent vision and stay calm in stressful situations. They can also live to 50 years old, rather than the 15-year lifespan of a dog. This means a guide horse can be a companion for most of a person's life.

However, unlike a dog, a guide horse cannot sleep inside and needs a stable to live in and a garden to run around in. They also have to be trained for one year, so they get used to responding to their owner's commands.

HEARING DOGS

For people who have difficulty hearing, a trained dog companion can make a big difference. Hearing dogs have been used for over 20 years.

Like a guide dog or horse, a hearing dog has a close friendship with its owner. The dog's first task each day is to nudge its owner awake when it hears the alarm clock go off.

It then alerts its owner to other everyday sounds, such as oven timers, smoke alarms and phones ringing. The dog can also lead its owner to someone who is calling from another room.

Hearing dogs also respond to door bells and take their owners to the door. Outside the home, hearing dogs alert their owner to sounds that indicate danger. This could mean stopping them from crossing the street in front of a car, for example.

PET THERAPY

Pets provide great company for people. They can also keep us calm. Scientific tests show that stroking a pet makes humans more relaxed. It can even improve our health.

Some pet owners take their animals to visit patients in places such as hospitals and nursing homes. These 'therapy pets' include dogs, cats and rabbits that are used to spending time with strangers.

The purpose of pet therapy is to help people cope with their health problems by making them forget their worries for a while.

People with physical or learning disabilities can visit pet therapy farms. Here, visitors hug lambs, feed cows, groom ponies and connect with animals in a countryside setting. Animals almost always make us feel good.

PULLING PLOUGHS

Since ancient times, animals have helped people with transport, travel and towing simple machines. In many places today, horses, donkeys and camels still carry people and their things from place to place. Other large animals help farmers in their fields.

In Southern Asia, oxen called water buffalo help farmers by pulling ploughs. A plough is a digging tool that prepares a field to be sown with seeds.

With their large hooves and flexible feet, water buffalo are perfect for ploughing the deep mud of rice paddy fields. A tractor would simply become stuck doing this work.

Oxen are strong, hardy animals that have helped humans for centuries with many different tasks. Oxen can plough fields, pull carts and tow large loads, such as fallen trees. Oxen are slow, patient creatures that can operate in both hot and cold climates. They continue to be partners to farmers around the world today.

PACK ANIMALS

From the Andes of South America to the Himalayas of Central Asia, many people live in high, mountain areas that are impossible to reach by car. Because roads are often just rough tracks, 'pack animals' such as donkeys, ponies, yaks and llamas are used to transport people and their things.

Donkeys are strong, sure-footed animals that can carry large loads up narrow mountain passes and down steep slopes. Donkeys were domesticated around 7,000 years ago and are social animals. Donkeys show little fear, but are also famously stubborn if they don't want to do something.

In the Andes Mountains, Bolivian salt miners use llamas to carry salt loads to the towns below. Llamas are calm creatures that can cope with high winds, frosty nights and scorching midday sunshine.

Llama hooves are perfect for mountain walking, but they will stand still and not budge if given loads that are too heavy.

CAMEL CARAVANS

Deserts are harsh, dry places where few animals can survive for long. To carry them across the vast, sandy dunes, many desert people rely on a perfectly-adapted animal: the camel.

Camels have tough, padded feet that can withstand the hot ground. To stop sand from entering their noses, eyes and ears, camels have thick eyelashes, hairy ears and nostrils that can clamp shut. They can also store food in humps on their backs and go for a week at a time without drinking water.

For centuries, camel caravans (a line of camels) have carried goods for people across deserts in Africa and Asia. But how does it benefit the camels?

Domesticated animals, such as camels, form a special bond with their human owners. In exchange for the animal's work, the owners provide food, water, shelter and protection against danger.

SLED DOGS

Arctic people and animals have to survive extremely cold, sometimes dangerous, conditions. Travelling by sled is a traditional way to get across ground covered in snow and ice. Several dog breeds are used to pull these sleds across this frozen terrain.

The Samoyed, Alaskan malamute and Siberian husky are well-known sled dogs. These dogs are friendly, confident and eager to run in a harness surrounded by a team of up to 16 dogs. The dogs have tough, webbed feet to run on the snow and can reach speeds of up to 40 kph. Their thick fur keeps out the cold and the dogs sweat through their tongues when they get hot. This prevents sweat from settling on the dog's coat and making it cold.

Sled dogs are working dogs that thrive on the exercise and excitement of pulling a sled. As pack animals, dogs are often happier when they can do a job together.

RESCUE HORSES

When there is an emergency or natural disaster, animal rescue teams are often brought in to help. After an earthquake, explosion or tornado, people may be buried in rubble. By using their super-sense of smell, animals can locate trapped victims.

The most common creature to find trapped victims is the sniffer dog. But there is another sniffing creature with an equally sensitive sense of smell and an even bigger nose: the horse. Because horses are large, they can easily sniff the ground and then lift their heads two metres higher to sniff above. This is a great advantage with ruined buildings that are still partly standing.

Horses also have exceptional hearing and can listen in two different directions at once. Their ears even point to where the noise is coming from, such as a person calling for help. Horses can also see well in low light conditions, allowing them to search at night.

MOUNTAIN DOGS

Mountains are extreme environments where conditions can quickly change. People sometimes become stranded in a blizzard, or trapped under an avalanche of snow. When these mountaineers are lost, rescue dogs are brought in to find them.

The typical dogs used for mountain rescue work include Bernese mountain dogs, Newfoundlands and St. Bernards, all of which are large, with thick fur for freezing conditions. But specialist 'avalanche dogs' are often smaller breeds, such as Labrador retrievers or Boykin spaniels. These dogs can sit on the shoulders of their handlers while they ski towards an avalanche site.

Once at the avalanche site, the dog sniffs the ground to pick up a human scent and then begins digging them out.

Dogs can search an area the size of two football fields in under 30 minutes and smell a person under four metres of snow. This is because dogs have 300 million scent receptors, compared to a human's six million receptors.

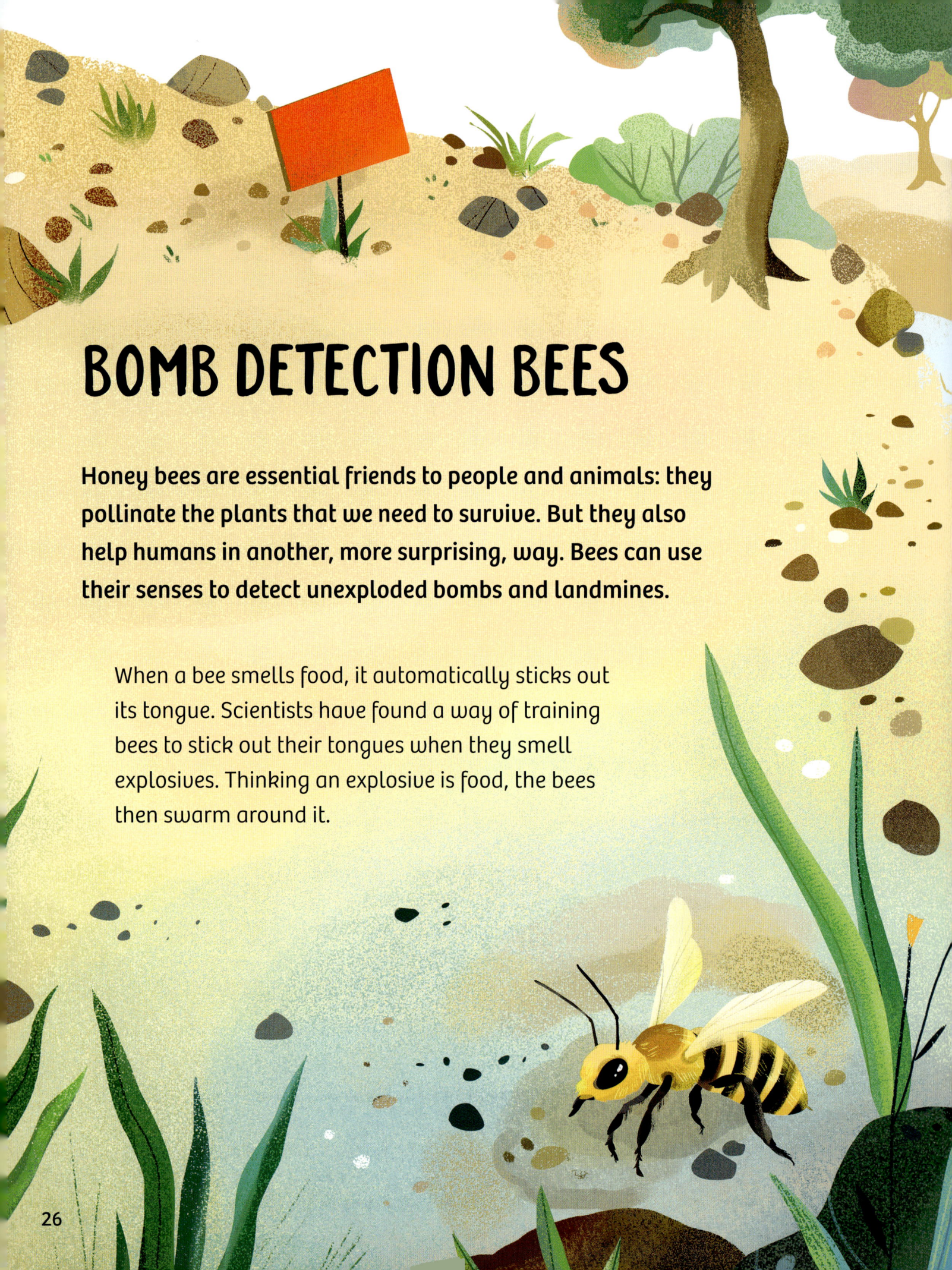

BOMB DETECTION BEES

Honey bees are essential friends to people and animals: they pollinate the plants that we need to survive. But they also help humans in another, more surprising, way. Bees can use their senses to detect unexploded bombs and landmines.

When a bee smells food, it automatically sticks out its tongue. Scientists have found a way of training bees to stick out their tongues when they smell explosives. Thinking an explosive is food, the bees then swarm around it.

This has made bees experts at finding landmines – a dangerous bomb buried underground which explodes when someone treads on it. But bees are too small and light to set a landmine off.

Uncrewed aircraft called drones have been used to track the bees and record any area they swarm around. The landmine is then removed and disarmed. Once their job is done, the unharmed bees are safely returned to their hives.

GLOBAL WARMING WHALES

Some animals have special abilities that can aid humans with scientific research. They can travel to places people cannot, or sense things that no human can see. These animals are helping us to detect disease, measure climate change and help us understand life in space.

One such creature is the narwhal, a tusked whale, which swims in the Arctic Sea around Greenland. Greenland is mostly covered by a vast ice sheet that is melting because of global warming.

Measuring this ice melt is important to understand how fast sea levels are rising. But freezing seas and treacherous icebergs make the area difficult for boats. Enter the narwhals.

Scientists have fitted narwhals with temperature sensors that measure the Greenland ice melt. Because narwhals dive to 1,700 metres under the Arctic ice, they can travel where no human can get to. The narwhal sensor data is then beamed to the surface. Best of all, no narwhal is harmed in the process!

DISEASE DETECTORS

People don't always know when they are sick. We can carry around some diseases for months without showing symptoms. But some dogs and rats can detect disease in humans with their sense of smell. And now, scientists think ants can become disease sniffers, too.

When humans have a disease called cancer, their urine, sweat and blood has a different odour. We can't smell the difference, but ants can.

Scientists have trained ants to sniff urine samples containing cancer, by putting sugar next to the sample. The ants learned that the odour meant food. They then picked only urine samples that contained cancer and ignored the others. Amazingly, it took only 10 minutes to train the ants.

Because the ants were so easy to train, scientists hope they will be used in the future to sniff out disease in hospitals. It could make ants one of the most important human helpers of all time!

SPACE ANIMALS

There are no animals living in space that we know of. But animals have been part of the human exploration of space since the 1940s. Today, they stay aboard the International Space Station (ISS) where they help us learn about living in space.

In 1960, the Russian dogs Belka and Strelka became the first mammals to orbit the Earth in a space rocket and return safely to Earth. The dogs were followed by an American chimpanzee, Ham, who went into space in 1961 before landing in the Atlantic Ocean. Ham retired afterwards to live in a zoo.

Ham's flight helped us to understand how lifeforms are affected by microgravity (very little gravity: the force that anchors us to the ground).

This work continued on the ISS. Here, spiders made odd-looking webs and fish swam in loops in their bowls. However, both creatures then adjusted to microgravity, giving us hope that humans could survive for long periods in space, too.

ALERT ANIMALS

We've seen many animals providing amazing help to human beings. However, there are still more animals that perform specific tasks. They are animal specialists.

Alert dogs help people with the condition epilepsy, which can cause seizures. During a seizure a person may feel sleepy, confused, or jerk around. A seizure alert dog is trained to notice a seizure taking place, and then help the owner. They may fetch medicine or a telephone, or direct the owner to a safe place where they won't hurt themselves.

Giant pouched rats are a special breed that can sniff out the disease tuberculosis and also landmines. The rats can detect tuberculosis samples in half the time it takes a scientist to test the samples.

They can also search an area the size of a tennis court in 20 minutes to find landmines. This would normally take a person with a metal detector four days to complete. The rats are too small to set off the landmines themselves.

HERDING DOGS

Dogs have helped farmers herd animals for hundreds of years. Dog breeds, such as Border collies, Australian cattle dogs and Blue heelers are experts in rounding up sheep and cattle and moving them from one place to another. They are often known as sheep- or herding-dogs.

Herding dogs are fast, intelligent, lively and able to understand complex instructions. A farmer may use hand or voice commands, or a whistle, to tell a dog to round up a flock of animals and move them from one field to another. Some herding dogs are able to move a flock simply by staring at them; other breeds bark and circle the animals.

Herding dogs love their work because they are helping their pack (in this case the farmer) and performing a similar task to their ancient ancestor, the wolf. However, unlike wolves, modern dogs are simply herding and not actually attacking the animals!

FERRET ELECTRICIANS

Laying electrical cables is a tricky job. It means pulling long electrical cables through narrow pipes, cramped wall cavities and under floorboards. Luckily, there is a skinny helper that loves scampering through small spaces: the ferret.

To help get electrical cables through long, winding pipes, a trained ferret worker is fitted with a harness. Attached to the harness is a long piece of very light, nylon line. Rope is attached to the nylon wire. The ferret then runs through the pipe with the light nylon wire. Once the ferret reaches the end, it is rewarded with a treat. People can then pull through the nylon wire, which pulls the rope to which is attached heavier electrical cables. Soon the cables are through the pipe, all thanks to our ferret friends.

Ferret electricians have had some famous clients. They threaded TV cables under St Paul's Cathedral in the UK for the 1981 wedding of Prince Charles to Diana Spencer. They did the same for the Millennium Eve concert at London's O2 Arena, which was then broadcast around the world.

ANIMAL PREDICTORS

We have seen that many animals have super-senses that are far more sensitive than our own. Some even seem to know when a natural disaster is about to strike, such as an earthquake.

Japan's Tashirojima Island is called Cat Island because it is inhabited by hundreds of cats, but only about 50 people. In 2011, the island cats suddenly snapped to attention. They began meowing loudly and the hair on their backs stood up on end. The people on the island noticed the cats strange behaviour and decided to take shelter.

Soon afterwards, there was an earthquake and the island was struck by a tsunami. The island harbour was completely destroyed, but no one died.

Experts think cats behave weirdly before an earthquake strikes because they can detect tremors in the ground that humans cannot.

ANIMALS HELPING ANIMALS

In this book, we've read about animals that help out humans. But what about animals that help other animals?

One example is the African oxpecker bird, which rides on the backs of zebras and wildebeests and eats ticks and flies from their coats. The oxpeckers then warn the animals that danger is nearby, by squawking loudly. In return, the oxpeckers get a free meal and transport.

Another example is the Colombian lesserblack tarantula and the dotted humming frog. Tarantulas normally eat frogs, but the dotted humming frog is allowed to live nearby and sometimes in the same burrow. This is because the frog eats ants and other insects that feed on the tarantula's eggs. In return, the tarantula protects the frog from hungry predators.

HUMANS HELPING ANIMALS

Where would we be without animal helpers? They are our home assistants, emergency rescuers and best buddies. Every pet owner knows what an important companion an animal can be. Animals can bring out the best in us and remind us to behave with compassion and kindness.

Just as animals help us, we can give back to them. There are many ways you can help animals. If you are getting a pet, you could ask to choose one from an animal shelter for abandoned pets. If you see an animal that is hurt or in trouble, you could ask an adult to help.

You can also remember to treat every animal with respect and lend a hand if it needs it. After all, humans are animals, and so we can be animal helpers, too.

GLOSSARY

Andes A South American mountain range that runs through the countries of Venezuela, Colombia, Ecuador, Peru, Bolivia, Argentina and Chile.

Avalanche A large amount of snow that slides down a mountainside.

Blizzard A long, severe snowstorm.

Companion A close friend that accompanies another.

Domesticated A wild animal that has been made tame to live around humans.

Independence To do something individually without relying on help.

Indicate Show, or point something out.

Impaired Something that is not working as it could.

Microgravity Being weightless because there is very little gravity to hold us down.

Landmine A bomb concealed under the ground designed to go off when a person or vehicle crosses it.

Predator An animal that hunts others to survive.

Receptors Groups of cells that help us sense things, such as sight and smell.

Toil Work hard for a long time.

Tsunami A giant destructive wave or series of waves often caused by an earthquake.

FURTHER INFORMATION

Books

Get Your Animals in Order by Michael Bright, Wayland, 2024

The Brilliant Book of Animal Bones by Anna Claybourne, Wayland, 2021

We Go Eco: The Animals We Save by Katie Woolley, Franklin Watts, 2024

Zainy, Brainy Animals: How Animals Communicate by Dr Ashley Ward, Wayland, 2024

Websites

National Geographic's all-things-animals website for children:

https://kids.nationalgeographic.com/animals

Natural History Museum website for children:

www.nhm.ac.uk/discover/british-wildlife.html

BBC Bitesize animal website:

www.bbc.co.uk/bitesize/topics/z6882hv

https://savethechimps.org/ham-space-chimp/

More about Ham the Space Chimp's incredible story

The Smithsonian Natural History website for children:

https://naturalhistory.si.edu/education/teaching-resources/life-science/early-life-earth-animal-origins

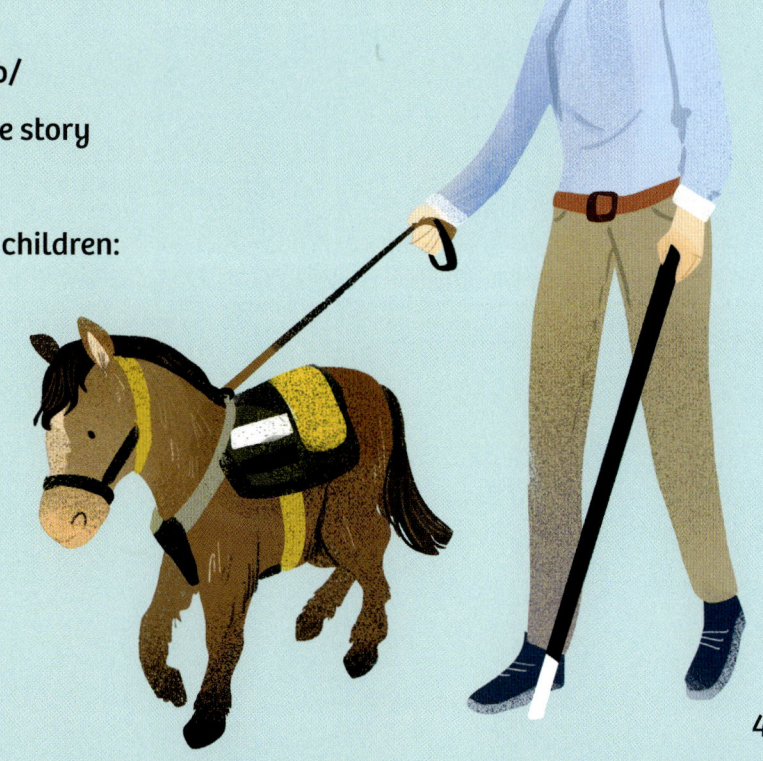

INDEX

alert animals 26–27, 34–35, 40–41, 42
animals helping animals 42–43
ants 30–31
Arctic 20–21, 28–29
avalanches 5, 24–25

bees 26–27
bombs 26–27

camels 14, 18–19
cats 7, 8, 12, 40–41
climate change 28
companion animals 4, 7, 8, 10, 44

deserts 18–19
disabilities 4, 13
diseases 5, 28, 30–31, 35
dogs 5, 6, 7, 8, 10, 12, 20–21, 22, 24–25, 30, 32, 34, 36–37
donkeys 14, 16

ears 4, 18, 23
earthquakes 5, 7, 20, 40–41
eyes 4, 7, 8, 18

farm animals 4, 13, 14–15, 36–37
ferrets 38–39

guide animals 7, 8–9, 10

hearing animals 10–11
herding animals 36–37
horses 7, 8–9, 10, 13, 14, 16, 22

llamas 16–17

mountains 16–17, 24–25

noses 18

oxen 14–15

pack animals 16–19
pets 4, 5–6, 11, 44, 45

rabbits 12
rats 30, 35
rescue animals, 22–25, 44
research animals 28–33, 35

senses, animal 5, 7, 10–11, 22, 23, 25, 26, 30, 35, 40–41
space animals 28, 32–33

tarantulas 6, 43
teamwork 6–7
therapy animals 4, 12–13
transport animals 4, 14, 16–17, 20–21

whales 28–29
wolves 6, 37